the eelgrass meadow

the eelgrass meadow

POEMS BY ROBIN CHAPMAN

TEBOT BACH • HUNTINGTON BEACH • CALIFORNIA • 2011

Cover art: Sea Grass & Shadows, 27″x40″, transparent watercolor by
                Lee Weiss, LEEWEISS.COM
Design, layout: Melanie Matheson, Rolling Rhino Communications

ISBN 13:   978-1-893670-79-2
ISBN 10:   1-893670-79-1

Library of Congress Control Number: 2011939878

A Tebot Bach book

Tebot Bach, Welsh for little teapot, is A Nonprofit Public Benefit Corporation which sponsors workshops, forums, lectures, and publications. Tebot Bach books are distributed by Small Press Distribution and Armadillo.

The Tebot Bach Mission: The mission of Tebot Bach is to strengthen community, to promote literacy, to broaden the audience for poetry by community outreach programs and publishing, and to demonstrate the power of poetry to transform life experiences through readings, workshops and publications.

This book is made possible by a grant from The San Diego Foundation Steven R. and Lera B. Smith Fund at the recommendation of Lera Smith.

www.tebotbach.org

ACKNOWLEDGMENTS

My thanks to the Banff International Research Station and the participants in its Creative Writing in Science Workshops, to Hilda Raz's master class at Taos, and to Susan Wicks and my manuscript groups for their wise counsel. I'm grateful to the Wisconsin Arts Board for a 2007 Literary Arts Fellowship that supported the opportunity to work on this manuscript and to the Banff Centre for the Arts for Leighton Studio residencies that provided quiet time and space to work on many of these poems; thanks also to Vermont Studio Center and Edenfred for their creative space. I'm also grateful to the following journals in which some of these poems first appeared, sometimes in slightly different form:

5 AM: "Marine Study Center."
Appalachia: "Architect of Desire," "End of March Again," "Lay-Over Day," "Sore-Eye Poppy," "Tents."
Ascent (online): "Cévennes, Vallongues," "Dark and Light," "What Luck."
Atlanta Review: "Strontium-90 After WWII."
Bellowing Ark: "Red-Spotted Toad."
Blue Unicorn: "The March of the Emperor Penguins."
Calyx: "Yangtze Basin River Dolphin."
Dalhousie Review: "Waves and Beaches," "The Harlequin Frogs of the Cloud Forest Preserve, Costa Rica."
Fiddlehead: "The Eelgrass Meadow."
Free Verse: "Brave New Biosphere."
Green Mountains Review: "The Heavy Metal Series: Uranium."
Hawk & Handsaw: "Reading the Science News to Escape the News."
The Iowa Review: "Rabbit Watcher."
The Journal of Humanistic Mathematics (online): "The Game of Life."
Locuspoint:Madison (online): "All That Breathing Out We Do," "Pygmy Hippopotamus."
Many Mountains Moving: "Cassandra Looks at Dark Matter Through Hubble's Eye."
Nimrod: "Praying to the God of Leavetakings."
Ouroboros Review (online): "Genevieve at Twelve Months."
OnEarth: "Joe's Dream."
Poetry East: "Field Sparrow."
Prairie Schooner: "Life in This Body," "Wanting the Moon."

Southern Poetry Review: "Time-Lapse."
Spillway: "Imagine."
Terrain (online): "Beginning Again in Banff."
Umbrella (online): "What Binds the Slime Mold Cells."
Valparaiso Poetry Review (online): "Provisioning, Moab, Utah."

"The All of It," "Brave New Biosphere," and "Praying to the God of Leavetakings" also appeared in the anthology *The Shape of Content* (C. Davis, M. Senechal, & J. Zwicky, eds.,Wellesley, MA: A.K. Peters, Ltd., 2008).

"Hometown" appeared in McAlister, N. & McAlister, Z. (Eds.) *Science Poetry.* Ontario, Canada: Neil Harding McAlister, 2011.

"One by One" appeared in slightly different form in the chapbook *Once* (Juniper Press, 2005).

CONTENTS

I. the eelgrass meadow

The Philosopher of Clear Sight

Four meters below sea level, Spinoza lives
      for seeing—grinds glass for spectacles
to return print and needlework
      to the old, breathes the fine dust
that will end his life as he polishes
      concave and convex lenses
and mirrors to collect and magnify starlight,
      focus the hairs of a flea,
bring to sight organelle and vacuole
      of creatures too tiny to see by eye.

And as he works and polishes, thinks
      on the God of all, the seen
and the unseen, the far-away and the near;
      extends light's transit
to the motions of hope and despair
      in the human heart,
moving in its attachments to the thought
      of the loved object,
its arrival, slow or quick, its steadiness
      or flickering, its loss—

thinks how God must be immanent
      in all of nature, ocean, each faint star,
with infinitely many other attributes
      we can't conceive or see,
so—no providential God, no immortality
      or rescue for us; for his heresies
excommunicated at 24 by the Portuguese Jews
      of Amsterdam, who don't want
more trouble than they already have—
      rivalries, the sea at their door.

He lives on milk soup with butter,
       gruel with raisins,
a daily pot of beer, spars
       with visiting philosophers,
keeps warm in bed writing up his analyses
       of *joy* and *sorrow, love* and *hope,*
like logical proofs in his *Ethics*—
       what he loves best is the thinking,
publishable only after he is dead.

Perspiculum √

Galileo, too, grinds glass spicule-
free from lumps
of heated sand, polishes to ripe
curve the objective lens, hollows a slump
of concave glass for the eye piece,
makes, from notes on Netherland's three-fold spie-
glass, a telescope he pumps
to twenty-power to harvest stars in a cloudy splice
of the Milky Way, craters pocking the Moon, moons slip-
ing across Jupiter's face: heretical sicle,
our earth-centered universe its purchase price.

Praying to the God of Spinoza

The child who takes sorrow to the woods
finds wolf-shadow pacing behind the trees,
phantoms of wind, ghosts of cloud,
or the trees themselves, ladders to sky,
bark a rough comfort, their branches arms—
from these small shifts a life plays out.

And life! What overlapping drench of dark
and light falls through the maple leaves,
what bright emerald shines on the back of the beetle
crawling through the musty leaf mold,
what elegant architectures of moss and fern uncurl
on stones beside the creek, or in the ice itself.

Here the equations of global change
alter ice to water, rainforest to sand,
in our calculus of money and oil that omits love—
we are another face of your face;
let us imagine you, original source, exact,
watching the unpredictable outcome
for all life's creatures
in the sunlight and dusk of this tiny blue ball.

The Hydra's Eye

Small freshwater jellyfish, first multi-celled creature to see,
    immortal, you carry still the change in protein code
        along your skin that prickles to sky's watery blue,

prey a shadow your mouth can taste the way our human infant's
    mouth opens to a nipple's brush today; and in our own eyes,
        simple protein switches, tuned through millennia

to catch sun's scattershot—morning sky, prairie green, berry-red
    in the feeding world as retina and compound eye evolve—
        watch how we have grown coupled

over the eons to this life through the light that reaches
    our eyes, how we have made, out of its reflected rays,
        the other's face, the architecture of rain,

the shape of each leaf, a world dizzy with creatures eating light;
    ours too the naming, its fumes of myth, the hero's task,
        the guardianship, the goddess's advice.

The Second Messengers ✓

Winged Hermes of the cell's crowded world,
small molecules suddenly sprung to life,
let out of school, or galvanized
to pass the word along at membrane walls,
drift through channels, mobilize
in watery interior slosh to knock, unlock,
grapple, tangle, tango, brush or push
the start of some local chemistry
to remake the path your day takes—

what do they shout, these short-lived
messengers silenced or corralled as soon
as they deliver their news? Tidings
from the world of nerves and gut—
neurotransmitters, histamines and hormones,
those cruise ships docked in the slips
of the cell's membrane, exotic arrivals
that send these messengers ashore
crying *run!*, or *help!*; or *something*

marvelous to eat is simmering on the stove,
or *the love of your life has arrived!* and then
the ponderous spools of DNA begin to turn,
start new proteins spinning, and all the business
of your life shifts—you set the table with stone-
ware and silver, sit down to dine on black-eyed
peas and hog jowls to welcome the new year,
offer the bowl of chopped green onions
to the man whom you will love for years.

When I can't sleep

at one or two in the morning,
    I leave your warm arms
        and the goose-down bed,
creep down the moon-lit stairs
    to the blinding light of the fridge,
        pull out the milk carton,
pour a cup by feel,
    thrust it, eyes closed,
        into the punched heat
of the micro-waved minute,
    fumble a capful
        of vanilla to add,
wander, wide-eyed,
    through dark shapes
        looming in the living room
to the windows,
    their friendly dark,
        waiting for the night world
to show itself—
    standing there, I've seen
        the silent winking
of lightning bugs
    rising in the locust trees,
        the sudden shadow
of a low-flying owl,
    February waddle of raccoons,
        racing rabbit pairs—
and each time, reassured,
    climbed the stairs
        to milky sleep.

Life in This Body   √

And those images of the brain lit up—
faces here, hand tools there, words heard,
words said, maps of the body, feet next to sex,
happiness glowing in the left frontal cortex,
grief with no words in the right, fear bright
in the amygdala, self here, consciousness
of self there, and mirrors of your mouth, hands,
movements everywhere, intention a latecomer—
what is it to live in this body, these bones,
the world entering in a river of light and sound,
smell of cut grass, gravity's tug?

Now the indigo buntings
are singing insistently in the walnut tree,
their flashes of metallic blue a color
that was never sky, and wild phlox the shade
of rainy cloud are releasing a perfume
that makes the bumblebees wild. Wind
gusts the daisy patch and green rises up
on a great scaffold of branches
into the building thunderheads.

All that pours in,
first spatter of rain, sound of your voice,
this inner life that is a singing underground—
who can point to bone or brain and say—
there's the river running through?

Portrait of the poet as a small ghost ✓

standing in light rain
wearing a white pillow case
down to her feet,
corners knotted for ears,
round Os
cut out for eyes,
larger Os for arms,
holding the handle
of a little red wagon
and her grandfather's hand—
Halloween, that new word,
the ceremony of standing
invisible in plain view.

And isn't this still true,
ghost calling to you
across invisible years
from the white blankness: O
see my grandfather's hands
that fed wild grapes
to the butterflies
and made willow whistles
as we walked through the woods;
see the rusting red wagon
of the world I loved!

What Binds the Slime Mold Cells ⚡

i.

The six legs of the fruit fly unfold
        from genes that made my own
                torso, fingers, toes—one ancestry.

The hunger that moves the foraging
        single cells of slime mold
                toward each other

to become one body rising out of soil,
        slug that travels, roots, fruits, dies,
                its spores an end to immortality—

what binds the slime mold cells binds me.

ii.

My ears that hear the seagull's cry,
                the wash of waves, footsteps in the grass,
                        miss the long low rumble of elephant calls,

the high insect-seeking chirp of bats—
                echoes making object of the world we find
                        through eye. Something enters and changes us,

and we find the world
                through which it comes as variously
                        as our need and history dictate,

each shaped by each.

iii.

At Churchill College dinner—long white table cloth,
                three wines—my seatmate tells me he's worked out
                        that it might have happened all at once.

A handful of molecules, water and rock,
        and all's begun—the strands that replicate
                themselves, their mirror opposites,

the host of protein products—once,
        in a lucky time and place, and life—our life—
                came tumbling forth, accumulating

improbabilities.

iv.

And that improbable common capsule
        the slime mold slug becomes,
                rooted on a slender stalk,

ripened spores cast out
        for another chance at life— we too
                in our common skin of atmosphere

move toward each other,
        invent the intricate moves
                that could make one body, delicate balance

of part for whole.

v.

Each inner world reports the outer one
        in shifting play of chemistry—
                what draws us forward in delight or need—

geese following and trading leads
        down the magnetic flare of sky,
                elephant caressing her mother's skull,

what rises in the apple tree,
        the fruitfly feeding on the apple,
                the fruitfly's memory of the tree—

what works in them, at work in me.

One by One

i.

Once, young and deep in first love,
   I walked Long Island Sound at night,
      hand in hand with him at the water's edge,

something running in me
   like high tide, pulling me into my life;
      I looked into the gray salt waves to see,

in their steep rise and fall,
   below the foam and breaking crests,
      deep in the body of the incoming sea,

thousands of coupling horseshoe crabs
   afloat in the sand-churned water,
      their armored bodies bronze and copper,

as though all the world were lovers,
   every being mated, there in the dark
      edge of the world.

ii.

And once, running alone in the Arboretum,
   I came on a leathery long-necked turtle,
      big as a platter

at the side of the road, digging
   into the graveled edge of asphalt
      beside Lake Wingra, her back flippers

scattering the hard-baked, stony soil.
   For the hour I stood there she dug
      and dug—the rest of the day, perhaps,

before she could lay her eggs and a night to cover them
       as bicyclists and roller bladers, cars and walkers
           passed her by—

no sign later of leathery eggshells
       or raccoon tracks, though now in every passing
           I wonder what is buried in the earth.

iii.

At the hill in Marquette County, after days of rain,
       I found earthstars somersaulting in the sandblow,
           starburst feet splayed open on the wet red sand,

and the field beside thick with spikes
       of purple blazing star, goldenrod,
           whorled milkweed, asters blue and white;

and came to the edge of the oak woods
       to find the earth itself pushed up
           into kingdoms of fungus and mushrooms–

fingers and scallops, castles and toadstools,
       fairy rings and oyster-white scaffolds,
           stippled oranges, purples, and blues.

And in another August, days of sun—a hundred degrees,
       milkweed and hawkweed withered and browned,
           woodland sunflowers seared to husk.

iv.

First summer, my first-born son held tight in my arms
       under my yellow poncho, we stood in a thunderstorm
           under the shelter, hail stoning the cedar shingles,

rain blowing in horizontal sheets. Hail the size
       of his fists lay thick among the battered penstemon
           and milkweed, the needle and Indian grass;

and later in the hammock under the oak leaves
　　　　we rocked in the sway and drip and wind-veer
　　　　　　　　rainbows of the weather's passing front.

I saw him there in his second year, stamping his foot
　　　　in a rainstorm's puddled mirror in the sand,
　　　　　　　　his face squinched shut for the gritty splash.

My second-born's face I saw emerge in the mirror
　　　　in the delivery room as I bore down and pushed,
　　　　　　　　and I knew him then for who he was.

v.

And once, hiking the winter oak woods, I saw, in every pane
　　　　of black ice, whole forests of ferns,
　　　　　　　　feathered trees and spikes flowered in crystal—

some swift shift of temperature that has not happened twice.
　　　　A time, on skis at Indian Lake, fat soft flakes
　　　　　　　　fell on the arched branches overhead, turning

the woods to lacy paradise; and a November hoarfrost
　　　　once, that turned the marsh to white–whole worlds
　　　　　　　　arising, flowering, melting away;

though the year of the ice storm, days passed
　　　　before it loosed its grip on branches, power lines,
　　　　　　　　every tree encased in glitter,

our roads black in the glaring sheen of ice,
　　　　so that we crawled on hands and knees,
　　　　　　　　clutching at frozen soil, breaking grass.

vi.

Once, walking the marsh edge on a June day,
　　　　where tadpoles had pooled the week before,
　　　　　　　　I saw the shallows alive with new frogs,

green and yellow-striped, so many that at my every step

dozens sprang up and disappeared into mud,
        reeds, cattail growth, the grass;
I thought there would be no end to them,
      the bounty that was life; though once, driving home
          through a mid-day dark as night,

tornado sightings thick on the radio,
      the road was slick with thousands crushed
          in crossing, hurled in a rain that would not stop.

We drove across their bodies
      in blackness, listening for the sound
          of funnel clouds tearing up the earth.

vii.

Each time I thought I had entered the ordinary world,
      that each season's turn would bring them back—
          that day, that sky, that ground,

moment by moment, slipping through my hands,
      the earth's rich abundance birthing, growing,
          vanishing; and something new

emerging–this day, your face,
      this once, each glimpse, every moment
          luminous; oh, how can we not kneel down,

and bless the ground?

Breathing

How was it, for those mammals
    mad with hunger and cold
        turning back again to the sea,

walking into the light-laced foam,
    into the surf
        clinking with ice,

after generations
    fishing along the shore
        when it was only another station

in the shambling prowl of bluff,
    blackberries, the upland meadows,
        the alpine flowers growing

small and close
    in the glacier's moving face?
        At least the layers

of salmon-fat
    beneath the fur,
        the fur that thickened

to twenty thousand hairs
    a square-inch—and the sharp teeth,
        and a tail

that could rudder in the current.
    And so it walked into the surf,
        walked deeper through tidal undertow,

where shellfish, gunnels, the pipefish hid,
    into the flashing roil of the herring ball,
        and opened its eyes and held its breath.

Waves and Beaches

-for W. Bascom

To watch the light traveling along the ocean crests,
the shadows criss-crossing in troughs,
and imagine motion traveling though time;
to translate motion to depth of water, current, wave—
to infer from these an island, seven thousand miles away:
cool respite for the mind
assigned to predict how the waves
from the H-bomb test would travel—
first the light that blinds, the x-rays that burn,
then the shock of the blast—then the deafening sound,
the island Elugelab, gone, a spreading plume,
Eniwetok atoll a torn wound. And if landslide,
the tsunami you computed beginning
its thousands of miles.

Will Safety be the Sturdy Child of Terror?

– Winston Churchill,
on the hydrogen bomb

Churchill's magnificent rhetoric
   put a positive spin—arms control—
on the weapon whose only purpose
   was to blow the world apart.
But let me ask you: would you build
   our children's future on a bomb
that could end our life on earth?
                     My field,
perhaps, no better, researching darkness
   in people's lives, the Black Dog
of Churchill's down days, by dropping
   baby monkeys down drains
they couldn't get out of, to show
   that it broke their hearts.

Who are the mothers and fathers
   of terror in this irrational world?
The primate monkey shakes in the corner
   of the isolate cage that Harlow built,
awaiting another inexplicable drop
   into funneled dark; despair,
the child of terror in this world.

The Whale Becoming the Angel of the World in the Field of the House

after Jo Going's 2-D sculpture & Pattiann Rogers'
poem, for my sister

How *whale*, descended from deer-like creatures
    walking backwards into water, bones
        submerged in fluke and flipper,
            buoyant blubber, holding breath

How *world*, in ocean's depths,
    but in the low, long songs
        that map the continental shelves,
            singing across space to kindred selves

In Baja's Laguna Bay, ten thousand
    grey whale mothers migrate, nudge
        their babies up to tourist rowboats—
            children of two worlds touch

How *whale*, when that other world's
    sonar blasts hemorrhage the inner ear
        listening for the whalesong in the house
            blue as iris field

Does the readback trace
    each small interior explosion?
        keep your voice down in the house
        whose house is it now

How *angel*, but in the lightness of play,
    flight along undersea currents,
        rising to spout in sunlit air
            remembering another world

carrying the body of the woman arriving
    to become the angel of our split-open world—
        look how her body emerges
            in the field of the water

Let the angel become the whale
　　　becoming the woman in the field
　　　　　of the encircling world, housed
　　　　　　　under a roof of stars

The March of the Emperor Penguins

Single file they cross the screen
on the hottest day of our summer,
a thousand black-caped creatures
heading into winter, wobbling side-to-side
like wind-up toys on bound feet,
belly-flopping when the ice slickens—
seventy miles from Antarctic water
to their breeding grounds.
In the dim theatre, we go quiet
as their silhouettes darken, teeter on.
Wind howls. Blue ice glitters
at 50 below and ice crevices open.
The line slows, detours, quickens
its pace. We can scarcely imagine
this way-finding, this night-and-day
marching under warping aurora,
the blizzards coming—though
the back-lit figures might be human,
might be us in some other time,
walking, tottering, never stopping.

Marine Study Center

You can touch them, the boy guide comes up
to tell me, showing me how, patting
the sea cucumber's rubbery mantle,
the thick stem of the anemone's flowered mouth.

This, he points to a short-armed starfish
glued to the edge whose skin I rub, smooth
and cool and slick. *It can make a quart of slime,*
he adds. I follow from open tank to tank

to hear what he loves—the moray eel's
charged presence, the retracting fringe
of the tubesnout, remembering this age in my sons,
the child's eyes looking out that still take the world

on trust—son who wrote, *I will go to school
like my dad, get a Ph.D.,* the summer before
his black-dyed Mohawk, the claws and skulls
and piercings of imagined blue tattoos.

I touch, and stroke, and hold those the boy says
I cannot harm, in coral, shell, or adolescent
camouflage. Tattooed on my son's torso now,
the bluebirds of happiness, the banners *hope and love.*

the eelgrass meadow

And what if we are no more than ribbons of grass,
          waving in the tide?
We could be an eelgrass meadow, subtidal zone.
          Our roots would clutch sand. Our leaves
would soften the waves, transmute sunlight to food,
          decay to a rich and rotting broth.
The larvae of ghost shrimp
          would browse among us, beginnings
of story; and in the dark abyss our bodies
          would nourish the rattail fish.
 If we were an eelgrass meadow,
          brooding anemone would grow to flower
their stinging barbs among us, the moonshell
          seastars would creep out into tidal pools.
The young salmon we sheltered would venture
          at last into the ocean's openness, travel
thousands of miles with the taste of our estuaries
          in their mouths to guide them home.

II. Homeland

Hometown

Which way was north?
Oak Ridge's directions were valley-skewed,
the long run of the road a compass needle.
The hills insistent
on the ways of water,
every fold a creek.

Which way was right?
The right was science-skewed,
the long miles of buildings
devoted to their task of sorting molecules,
pulling the small handfuls of death
out of the tons of yellowcake.

Which way was left?
What's left was mercury running into the creek,
the long mile of river, the roots of the trees.
What's begun always has its own logic,
runs like a clock, like stockpiles,
keeping them up.

Which way was true?
The long run of childhood was twilight
and heat, summer shimmering in the concrete pool.
The game had rules—not to be found,
and the black widow spider
another neighbor we knew to give space to.

Which way was danger?
The spider's eye refracted the high tension towers
that carried the power of the Tennessee River in flood
to the task of making nuclear weapons.
Here the intent to save
the world.

Which way was love?
At the Overlook, in old cars,

we kissed and kissed, the body's pull
an insistence—sap and root,
another place to view
the only home we knew.

Strontium-90 After WWII

-for my father

What came after you wrote this radioactive isotope
into a model of limits to the number of nuclear bombs
we could set off at once, seeding the shadow
of fallout, half-life a quarter century?

Project Sunshine, run by Army empiricists,
looking for signatures of strontium-90
in the bones of newborn dead, stillborn babies,
6000 shipped from around the world to measure

exposure in leg bones and backbones. There,
the cumulative record of 800 bomb tests pluming
the troposphere, fall-out carried around
the earth, raining down on all of us,

children's bones on which was built
an argument for test ban treaties, an end
to above-ground testing—the never-lived,
burned to fragile ash for a phoenix world.

The Bank of Violets

When at last my mother found the courage to admit
my father had left for good two years before
and wasn't sending for us even with a job in hand,

when she saw that she had to learn stenography
and qualify as a fifth grade teacher and single-parent
and leave the apartments where Union Carbide

housed us according to our temporary rank,
she went to the bank with her school-teacher's pay
and mortgaged our future for a new pre-fab

built on Robertsville Road, west edge of town, first
houses that an Oak Ridger could own, ours at the head
of Salem Road, backed by a twelve-foot bank of violets

and four towering maples that had once been a farm
seized for the frontier-town's secret growth—
small box of house but our own, and builders would add

another room, the creek ran nearby, the apple orchard
bloomed, and she promised us the bank of violets, where
tender ephemerals, Mayapples, hepatica, phlox

would light up our morning breakfasts of broiled
butterscotch toast, our scramble to find books and coats
and catch the new bus to a new school.

She painted our future as the developer, in one last pass,
brought in the bulldozer to scrape the topsoil off the lots.
Gullies ran red down the raw clay bank as we moved in

and tears streamed without stop down our mother's face
as she looked at the eroded slash that would be our view
from the dining-room's picnic table, rough-hewn boards

that physicist friends had hacked from soft pine;
for twenty years she rose at 6 a.m. to replant violets
as best she could in the rocks and the subsoil.

The End of Biology

Inductees, we studied vision and locomotion in the lab,
jewel-green yellow-and-black-spotted leopard frogs
colored for marsh marigold and cattail camouflage,
and the instructor wanted us to record the impulses
that flashed behind their eyes when flies darted past,
that link between the eye and tongue that feeds hunger
and keeps them agile in the round of life, for which purpose

we were to paralyze the frog, tuck cotton balls
under its tongue, and maneuver the fly speedily
across its view in convincing bursts of flight,
adjusting electrode leads and tuning in the static
of neurons on oscilloscope screen—this may have required
(the mind refuses to recall) electrode needles
implanted, painlessly we were assured, in the pool

of neurons that report flies in the frog's private world,
and we did all that and saw– yes– the tongue
is connected to the eye, but to end the experiment
we were taught to pith the frog, sharp needle
to scramble the brain above the spinal cord
and study the leg muscles, that would twitch
when we zapped the nerves, movement just a reflex.

I quit the major, wanting to know what fly veer
and sun dazzle, cool muck and frog song, meant to the frog,
not how to curarize, chloroform, pith, and dissect.

Rabbit Watcher ✓

In a Welsh malt-house converted to cabin I'm reading the 1964 classic
by R.M. Lockley, true British eccentric who spent his years up a tree,
spying on rabbits' social networks, their wars over warrens, their digging
and tunneling, grazing and cropping, courting and sleeping, breeding
and greeting, sunbathing, fighting, marking their corner of island territory.
He even describes, *Deus ex machina*, how he ruined a life to satisfy
curiosity, moving the Head Rabbit out of his green kingdom
for three long weeks—time enough for Shakespearean plot to evolve,
for the Queen to take up with an upstart Pretender who moved in,
sent the old King, returned to the field, into life on the margins of the down,
grazing thistles and scuttling out of the path of former sycophants,
his fur matted and ungroomed, his eyes dark and wild. And Lockley—
living on a small island overrun by 10,000 rabbits—tries infecting them
with Australian rabbit fever, follows up with cyanogas in all the warrens
and burrows. Takes up bird-watching, making life lists, identifying gulls.

Discovery Channel

The behavioral scientist pats the dog on her lap, explains
to the camera, *We don't know whether animals have emotions.*
The Airedale's ears cock. He pants, drops his jaw, wags his tail
as her hands stroke his wiry coat, looks her in the eye.

We need to experiment, she insists to the viewing audience;
chickens for instance; *we get chickens to calibrate
for us in pecks which mash they most prefer, whether
they want grass or wire mesh underfoot.* I watch the chickens
vote determinedly for solid ground and lettuce; impatient, start
to click her off,

     but Jane Goodall comes up next, casually cuddling
a chimpanzee infant. Goodall bends her own head for its mother
to groom. I think of Harlow's infant monkeys raised with wire-mesh
or terry-cloth mothers or none, as if a mother were a texture;
their years of shaking isolation after. Of Washoe, the chimpanzee
raised to sign, who signed 'rock baby' over her stillborn infant.
Of how much more there is still to learn.

Architect of Desire

I come upon him in rainforest dawn,
glossy black bird, unmarked, assembling
on the straw of his courting floor
the objects to catch his lady's eye—
litter of tent scraps, clothespins,
and tobacco blooms all smoky blue;
and the yellow gold of strawflowers
and crumpled candy bar wrappers, scattered
on the carpet of leaves about his bower
of sticks and twigs, an upswept U
where he will wait for her
at dawn, at dusk. And what I think
is how for them it must still
be the same old love or longing
for these exact shades of blue and gold
that lead each to find the other
in the Bowerbird's rainforest courtyard.

Brave New Biosphere

The pieces are in our hands—the four-letter code,
        the genomic list—here's you, here's me,
each of us thirty-five thousand genes on the microchip.
        Why not augment ourselves? Add the prey-stunning
electrical cells of the eel to the human arm, bioluminescent
        eyes for the dark from the ocean depths,
plant chloroplasts that allow our skin, green now, to feed
        on light. No need for food, or transit, or oxygen;
we could stand about in the future, ferny-fingered by day,
        flashing our glowworm codes by night,
needing only filamentous, permeable feet to bring water,
        a waxy skin to shed wind and mosquitoes,
a little space in the fattening light. Tended, if we were lucky,
        by gene-altered trees grown muscular and agile
on actomyosin, shuffling along on knuckled roots, responding
        to our chemical signals of blossoming or distress
in the greenhouse gas; and if the changing shape of our future
        makes us as silent as bristlecone pines, oh leave us
those cheerful and modest descendants of dinosaurs, the birds.

The Game of Life √

Not the children's game of chutes and ladders
but the mathematician's toy of rules and repetition,
model of a world whose cells will toddle through
successive states of on and off, life and death, evolve
into the steady states of blocks or beehives, boats,
or blink endlessly in patterns we name beacons,
pulsars, toads—or else the future zips across
our screen like spaceships passing—
gliders, glider guns,

                          unless it all blinks off.
The game a matter of John Conway's simple rules:
your neighborhood a grid of three by three,
you a cell who can be born
if exactly three neighbors already live;
if fewer than two exist, you die
of loneliness; if more than three, you die
of overcrowding, event repeated across the board—
birth and death,
                   but no love or mourning,
no gold-winged warblers moving through the rain,
no redbud bursting its bark to flower, no wild leeks
simmering, no way to knock on a stranger's door.

Following the Cathar Martyrs of Southwestern France, 1202-1244

Tourists, we stare up at Montsegur, last retreat of the Cathars, sect fired
by belief in earthly evil and heavenly good: why
would a god have made this imperfect world with its tainted air,
venal men, muddy rivers carving karst and earth,
hidden caves of phallic stones and ochre-smeared thighs? Not
the God of Paradise, perfect in his celibate joys and crystal waters.

And when the Crusaders starved them of bread and water,
built below their fortress a pyre to put an end to heresy, set fire
to light their way to Judgment, not
one of 225 escaped, or tried; why,
when half a million of them already lay slaughtered under the earth?
They marched down into that bonfire singing airs.

Night, and no more hope of life than air
in that inferno, and no hope of water
to mix with vinegar, no smothering earth—
passion burned on all the faces, fire-
lit, those marching into flames, those waiting. Why
think of the powerful who sent the orders, what the few not

there set burning: the tortures of inquisition not
extinguished yet, and the land seized by the winners, heirs
by force. Those walking into fire knew why
they entered a better world; their faces glowed with the sweat
of hereafter, the holy roar of new-caught fire
that burned to smolder, ash, scorched and sterile earth.

Those standing there to guard their faith knew earth
would receive all, soon or late, and sort the chosen out; not
this world but the next was where one feared eternal fire.
They fixed their pikes and wound rags to shut out the choking air,
wiped their sweating horses down with water,
asked who and how and where and when but never why.

They knew: *For our country. For our faith.* And why,
the words still ringing, do we believe life on this earth
can alter? We walk the caves cut by water,
the guide's light flickering over the knot
of horses drawn by an artist's hand 12,000 years ago in icy air—
no hell, but creatures birthed in an oil lamp fire.

At Montsegur, the newest fortress weathers; we ask, why not
embrace all our elements? Earth spins, wrapped in its fragile air;
the cave horses drawn by fire-light run the paths of water.

Legacy

Now fragments of bone and ash in the Bay you loved,
Father, what did you teach in our few visits?
Cook rice with onions, drink your martinis dry,
watch out for the jib, the sawdust, the jig,
take the man's arm when you cross the street;
actions imply values, you said, *never embed*
an infinite series in a finite model, take the whole
to the limit instead.
                                    But scale,
I sputter, scale matters if human life is the measure,
if sons and daughters count, there may not be time
enough in a life to find answers! you'd nod, I imagine,
point out that sometimes we solve the problems we can,
not the problems we need to. You told the war machine
long ago: too many bombs at once would kill us all,
and still they crank them out.
                                    I wave the equations
of chaos to say, models will never be enough;
even simple determinism may not know
what comes next—Eden, apocalypse, a mix;
you'd agree, I imagine, but say *life is finite,*
like the model, tell me *what the hell, live, lighten up.*

Wanting the Moon

Mother gone to dust, some
    flower bed where
        impatiens brightly bloom,

Father an ash sunk
    through the waves,
        water in your bones—

what story of loss
    am I inventing
        in this perishable world?

Both of you woven
    in the fabric
        of my every cell,

irritable argument and soup
    simmering on the stove,
        love dining at the table,

small birds waiting
    for handouts as you
        disappear into the new—

every morning will wake to hunger.
    Every evening will close its wings, fed,
        whether the moon is dark or full.

Dark and Light

Walk through the woods at night in the dark,
no moon, no light from the city reflecting white
on the clouds that hide the stars—foolish to do
except you discover that degrees of dark will mark
the path, the opening in the canopy, the rise
and dip of rock and ditch, the fallen log—through
the vast spectrum of energy's frequencies some few
still reverberate in the retina's rod-packed back,
translating world into dark-darker-darkest yet:
and this, though you do not call it that, is light.

How We Know What We Know

The girl in the bookshop, telling
        how she offered her sheaf
of words to the teacher
        who brushed them off,

sent them flying like leaves into the current,
        her silence that followed after
a hunger to be heard
        by a fellow creature—

the blind woman fingering Braille,
        the girl in pink tights
checking text on her iPhone,
        the man tuned to talk radio—

each of us listening, listening,
        for a voice we know.
What did she tell us,
        that girl in the bookstore,

who might have been myself,
        green girl studying botany
and the modern philosophers,
        writing songs for epistemologists,

words flown now into the rain,
        detritus of speech
falling into the stream that is life
        running through us?

Say that we are the shaded banks of the river
          with their histories of mud
and mink, that we are trout lingering
          in sinkhole shadows for minnows,

say that we flow through the world
          through the niches between
the makers and drivers
          of loud-voiced machines

that move earth and its boulders
          to build a bridge or dam up
the river, that lift their whirling blades
          into currents of wind.

Say that we sing the river,
          our whispers of breath
through the mist
          stirring the hair-cells

of the coiled cochlea,
          resistance repeating the sounds
to heart, rock, root:
          say that we learn by feel.

III. Canyonland Country

Canyonland

How to go into a lunar landscape,
thread of a river the only green;
how to live where there's no food
or clean water, where canyons
are swept by flash floods
and sandstorms scour the rock face
and heat sucks the skin dry;
how to follow our hearts
into a desert place? We who are
so small, and mostly water,
with bones that break—what
will we learn from the red rock?

Provisioning, Moab, Utah

Tradition, to stop here on the way
to the Green, provision
with sweet water from rock.
A faucet set in the canyon face
runs without ceasing, no handle
to turn it off.

We fill up every bottle,
bucket, jug, and water bag,
lug the precious gallons counting—
eleven days on the desert river,
seven of us, a gallon a day for each.

We handle the soft plastic bags
like babies, lay them
carefully side by side, watch
as dry air and sandstone
suck up moisture till we're sure
no seal leaks, no pinhole drips—
this day and this day and this day
for each of us.

Though ten years later
when we stop again,
the stream's a drip;
the aquifer dried up.

Natural History

The Green River snakes a brown-gold
      path through Utah's rock,
cutting through 200 million years—ocean floors,
      lake-beds, dunes, mud-flats, dust;
sediment pooled, compressed, collapsed,
      eroded, wind-sheared,
marsh-clumped—fragments recomposed,
      like any story, into a fiction—
the age of dinosaurs, of ferns,
      verging, now, on the brachiopods.

And our small pods of canoes,
      heaped with nine days' gear
pulled armthrust by wristflick
      through the cold silted river—
we, too, make history
      laid down in the riverbed
stroke by stroke, the eddies after,
      slip by slip on the risky shore,
patch by patch of tent footprint,
      step by step in the cryptogamic soil.

Our lives here briefer
      than the red-spotted toad's,
we with no belly-skin to breathe the water,
      not enough torpor to burrow into mud.
Like the small red lizards, we hunt out
      shadows and overhangs
to shade our meals of nuts and berries,
      powerbars and cheese.
Like them we move to heated stones
      as dusk comes on,

claim our place for night
      under a jagged sky we once named
Heaven's Dome, wheeled by Scorpio, Sagittarius,
      Orphiuchus, Cygnus the Swan—
watch meteors streak the Milky Way,

the old light of stars arrive,
red-shifted as they spiral into hungry dark;
        drowse under a soft rain of neutrinos,
gamma rays, x-rays, photons of every age
        through the jittery flights of bats.

The Heavy Metal Series (Uranium)

Weightiest of heavy metals, Uranium
        lies buried along Utah's rivers
in a brown strip of Moenkopi time laid down
        in Triassic years,
red rock country now, mined
        to yellowcake ticking its unstable
life away—twelve million tons
        of tailings drip from the unlined
pond by our Moab campsite
        into the Colorado, the groundwater,
lacing the mesclun organic mix,
        the Phoenix reservoir
where my jazz bassist son on subsistence
        gigs buys bottled reverse-osmosis
drinking water—
                and most of the yellowcake
        separated now, in the Tennessee town
I grew up in, into the fractions
        for nuclear weapons and reactor fuel,
the spent fuel recycled
        as depleted uranium hardening
the DU bullets that litter the sands
        and streets of Iraq
to armor-piercing strength, *depleted*
        meaning only as radioactive as X-rays,
uranium another heavy metal
        binding to the DNA, destroying life;
death in a handful of molecules
        pulled from the thin snaking line
that Navajo elders refused to mine, death
        in a litter of bullets for surviving children
to play with—look what we've found, buried
        in earth and freed, this handful of dust
running through our fingers.

No knowledge that we will not seek,
no instrument that we will not use,
no frontier that we will not cross,

no blueprint that we will not build,
no weapon that we will not sell,
no law that says learn the cost first,
no model that predicts the real.

Here we are, death on our hands, paddling down
        a wilderness river, deep in Canyonland country,
knowledge the only way out: better
        look down river than up
to chart a course, unless we're checking weather.
        Who will be the keeper of clean water?
Who will be the keeper of clean air?
        Who will be the keeper of the lizards,
canyon wrens, and scorpions? Who will be
        the keeper of cottonwoods and cactus?
Who will be the keeper of our food, our boats;
        who will be our maker of maps?
Who will lift our spirits? Who will bag and carry
        out our trash, and where will we put it?

Schooling

We learn to watch out for the slowest,
the weakest, the unschooled, the scared—
the one who is still learning to paddle,
the who has never put up a tent,
the one who wanders off.

Will shows me the power stroke,
how to use my back, flip my wrist,
relax; how to ferry across in swift current;
how to watch for the slick clay, getting out.
Next day we keep up.

I learn the work—how to unload the gear,
how to pitch and strike the tent, where
to put the port-a-potty, the drill for washing dishes.
How to keep cool, dipping my clothes
in the river. The rhythm of packing up.

We read aloud Abbey's story
of trying to talk home the wild horse.

Tents

Thin nylon skin of orange and yellow,
mesh that grids the canyon face to pixels,
plastic floor set between our sleep and sand,
between our limbs and scorpions or ants—
home, we call it, set up every afternoon
when we unload canoes, make camp—rehinge
aluminum poles on their stretchy ropes,
thread them through the tent sleeves,
inflate the space we carry with us—
then to anchor it, stakes weighted with rocks,
roped to tree or outcrop—unzip, unroll, inflate
the Thermax pads, lay out the flannel sheet,
fluff up the splayed-out sleeping bag,
bundle our jackets of fleece for pillows,
turn to each other before we sleep—

though Jim, alone, climbs up to the mesa top,
sets down his pad and sleeping bag,
takes the night sky for his house.

All Night in Trinalcove Canyon, the Wind

pours without ceasing over damp skin;
it could be water slipping over our shoulders,
eddying around breasts and bellies, cool water
ladled over our faces, trickling through lips,
eyelids; whispering into my ear; lifting my hair;
it could be your own touch, this delicate tracing
of every crevice and surface— the wind's voice,
stone-warmed desert canyon vortex, pours
through tent mesh, sighs through night sky,
leaving our heat-stunned flesh salty and cool,
moves on to shake the leaves of the cottonwoods
like castanets, making the sound, all night,
of rain, falling endlessly into our sleep,
drumming through our red-rock dreams.

Red-Spotted Toad

Canyonland, Utah, 2004

In hot noon by the plunge pool's scummy brown-green,
        you shine like wet black mud, jasper-glinted,
smaller than my little finger. Your dark tadpole brothers
        and sisters, sides swollen with gills still,
wiggle at the pool's edge, eyes full already of rock, sky, sun
        at the amphibian edge of membranous water.

Gail looks up your small mud-splat shape in the field guide—
        tells us you can wait months for the brief desert pools,
breathing and drinking mud and dew through your skin, buried
        through the baking sun's drought, the cracking of earth,
desiccation of self—lose 40 percent of your own body's water,
        and hold on till the crack of lightning over the mesa

spills thin threads of rain, trickles of water. Some trail
        overhead, a veil; some descend. Rivulets
soak soil crusted by cyanobacteria and fungi,
        run on, gathering speed, force, water, stream
to the canyon lip, pour off in waterfalls after the shower,
        swell the pool where you will hear the high musical trill

that calls you out of mud to mate, lay the jellied eggs
        that grow to tadpoles in a few hours, dwell in the potholes,
climb, now, out of the shrinking pool to wait. Those who stored
        grain in cliff-rock shelters here 800 years ago, only handholds
and footholds for access—how long did they last
        through that drought of seventy years?

Sore Eye Poppy

Look but don't touch, says its name—*sore eye
poppy* blooming next to a petroglyph wall
in its own history, old stems golden and stiff
at the bottom of the bush, linear grey-green leaves
and seedpods in its rising circle of brush,
round buds and orange-scarlet flowers borne
on the top—a globe rising, flowering,
fruiting, falling away.
All around an empty space
signals where roots have searched.

At night in its bowl-shaped blossoms
small bees sleep curled in its scent,
unstung by the fine gray fuzz of star-shaped hairs
that sting the hand or mouth that picks it—
how every desert flower finds a way
to say *come hither—keep away.*
Would we, in a harsher world,
grow as prickly and beautiful
in the wreckage of our days,
as tender at night to the bees?

The Invention of Writing √

Those secret marks on stone, red-ochre hands,
carvings on bone, knots in rope,
petroglyphs, pictographs, runes,
pottery shards, alphabets holding the play
of tongues: any one of us would have done it
to carve our name, mark solstice,
name the plants for bone-ache, migraine,
death, or sacred vision; scratch
a tally of grain stored in the canyon walls;
for those too shy to speak, a way to be seen.

Lay-Over Day

We watch the Green River, only road here, rise three feet—it covers the rock that caught and held our friend Anka yesterday, as the water swept her away from shore—only a dip in the brown waves now, a spill of eddies below. Rolland and Will tossed her a rope, river mermaid, pulled her back to shore. Only afterward saw how there would be no going back in the spring flood.

Fire-blackened logs, sticks, debris churn past, bobbing, rocking in the current's race. The honey-salt scent of tamarisk, its pink-white fronds of blossom wind-whisked, drifts. Wasps crawl through the Gambel oaks. Spiders string silk along all their rough bark. Swarms of gnats eddy about the deep-lobed green leaves. Brown river foam sparkles in the river's wake.

Across the river and behind our tents, Wingate sandstone towers for hundreds of feet, the lower talus slopes and scree in grey-green Chinle. All day, under the oaks, we read. Sound bounces back: the raven's croak, the scrape of a canoer's paddle against a gunwale long before he comes in sight. Joyce turns a page in the heat. Sand scatters as a spotted lizard, beige and rust, runs past the water can.

A hundred and five degrees in the shade. The lizard runs up the trunk of the oak, stares at our friend Jim as he waves a dry twig to catch its eye, slips his other hand behind the trunk to catch its tail. Working hardest is the parasitic wasp, digging sand trails, a hole, hauling black flies to its mouth, another generation to feed now. Wind rustles the leaves of the Gambel oaks.

A hiss, as John opens the lunch bucket, releases the sharp spice scent of sausage, our mouths suddenly wet. Descending trill of a canyon wren. Constant bee hum. Dry slither of a yellow-striped garter snake.

Someone rises, moves a canvas camp chair back into the moving shade. On the walls of rock, deep red desert varnish traces the path of rain, spalls and flakes to pink-orange face.

Evening; red and blue enter the river, repeat the rock and the sky.

IV. Old-Growth Forests

Charles Robert Darwin and Marianne North Encounter the Rainforest √

He saw that St. Paul's Rocks
    were populated first by
the booby and noddy—*not*
    a single plant, not even
a lichen—but crabs in the rocks,
    a fly and a tick
on the booby, a small brown moth
    that feeds on feathers,
a beetle and a woodlouse
    from beneath the dung;
spiders sailing silk—whatever
    could fly or hitch a ride
in the rich diversity
    of animal life.

And when he came upon Brazil's
    rainforests, vines growing
upon epiphytes growing upon
    live trees growing upon
the trunks of fallen trees,
    he wrote down the fauna he saw—
Maned Three-toed Sloth, the Golden-headed
    Lion Tamarin, but fell
speechless before the riot
    of green where no species
of tree repeated in any square mile,
    where sun fed flowering carnivores,
wrote in the Beagle's journal
    only *Transports of pleasure,*
pressed leaves to send back
    and catalogue.

She traveled years later, his letters
    of introduction in hand,
with her brushes and box of oils for company—
    viridian, ultramarine blue, yellow ocher,

alizarin red—to paint, species by species
        in their own habitats,
passionflower, palm tree, *Scadoxus multiflorus,*
        showing what words can't tell:
shadow and light, reflection, refraction,
        iridescence, the camouflaged
gestures of branch and leaf; returned
        to hang more than 800 paintings,
none sold, in a gallery she paid to have built
        in Kew Gardens, where the walls
still record orchids and creepers, trees
        and vistas of a vanishing world.

Edge Effects in Old-Growth Forests

Checkerboard clearcuts
strip the Pacific northwest.
          The Douglas firs left,
          over five-hundred years old,
begin to die back
at the new edges of meadow.
          Even as blueberries take hold
          and the black bears forage,
the microbial net
shrivels to dust,
          sun like a knife
          slashing through forest.
What is interior?
The mind partitions its world,
          slop and slosh of nutrient broth
          in the root,
bang of blood
in the temple and wrist,
          red blood cell ferrying its four oxygens
          to heart, brain, stomach, feet;
six-eight-nine billion hearts
pumping and pumping
          CO_2 out at the bottom
          of the oxygen-rich atmosphere,
mist rising to rain
from old-growth conifers
          for a little time yet.

Ida (*Darwinius masillae*)

…this is our Mona Lisa, Jon Hurum,
Oslo University's Natural History Museum

A missing link? Small lemur-like primate,
only her just-discovered bones remain,
her baby teeth, the hairs that covered her
body, the remnants of a meal. Her broken
wrist is beginning to heal, preserved
these 47 million years at the bottom
of Messel Pit, shale sediment of a lake
where she must have ventured
for a last drink—and then the belch
of suffocating volcanic gas, the tumble
into history—

        but she has no grooming
claw, no teeth comb, so perhaps she's ours—
first ancestor of the lineage that evolved
through Africa and Asia into Leonardo's
dextrous hand, Mona Lisa's enigmatic
smile.
      Or no, measurements show
she's another line, dead-end, extinct,
written out of ancestral story and into
a modern one, of human need for hype,
a paleontologist in a vodka bar
looking at Ida's photo over his drink.

In either case, her permanent teeth
were just beginning to come in,
and her wrist ached, and she was thirsty.

Large Black Slug
(Arion ater)

Black as wet anthracite
in rain-drenched grass,
black deepened to wrinkled,
iridescent velvet
with the green-flecked shine
of emerald bottle glass,
mantle smooth, one lung-hole
and underneath a net of blood

to take in breath
on the Welsh bridle path
among the litter of lichen
and hedgerow leaf
the waning moon and mud
of equinox night
as we light our way over stones
and stiles, stepping to miss

this small muscled foot,
horned blind feelers
and unblinking eyestalks,
stretching forward all mouth
to feed and find a mate,
traveling on her-his own slime—
where does the body end
and locomotion begin?

Feeling and seeing and
knowing and action
slip seamlessly past
Aristotle's analytical ax,
Plato's ideal categories,
Descartes' extended thought,
the slug sliding on the heat
of its own making,

happy in the wet ooze
of moonlight and detritus,
carrying eggs
of a mirrored lovemaking,
gluing the coiled calcareous
coracle shells
of the next generation
to the stones that will shelter them

in a line laid down
before Druid days—
Will and I slog on past rabbit holes,
startle a rookery of birds,
send badger scurrying dimly
down the path,
trusting in the ways laid down
in the hedged and tunneled world.

Day-Hunting Dragonflies

We see you hovering like helicopters over the standing waves
of Boundary Waters whitewater,
but you've seen us
long before—

your eyes like doubled helmets merging what enters 30,000 lenses
from every direction
and all of above,
below.

What do you see with those five color receptors taking us in?
Green body
of our canoe, sweep
of orange paddles

like a giant dragonfly, under a sky compass flickering at dusk
with polarized light
that orients
wilderness,

sky-blue shot through with the brightness of indigo, violet, UV
that we can't see,
highlighting every
water nymph,

each mosquito wingbeat, three hundred times a second,
hovering over
that mosaic
our bodies make.

Imagine

If you were small and young,
thrust outside to make your way
in all weathers,
your companions scattered
over the wide sky,
the endless hunt for food and shelter,
the blind journey on the back of the wind
for hundreds of miles—
how the huddled warmth
of the remembered nest, down breast,
beakful of food answering
your frantic calls
would sustain and keep you now.

Cévennes, Vallongues

So this was paradise: wild boars roaming the chestnut woods,

scent of truffles deep in the soil, sky a Mediterranean blue,

the wild trees dropping fruit—cherries, olives, apricots—

into our hikers' hands, sweet water springing out of the rock,

each deep fold of hill speaking another rushing dialect.

Place where life retreated as the glaciers stopped.

We stop by a farm for three kinds of chèvre where goats

crop oregano and thyme. In the hayfield, a donkey twitches flies

with his ears and the shepherd plays the flute to his dog

under the scent of the linden trees, buzz of black bees.

Out of the land's shattered schist, mile on mile of rock

terrace the steep fields of wheat, stack up to make walls

for houses and barns, everything needed at hand: before

the Picts, the Goths, the Celts, the Roman aqueducts—

stone and honey, bread and cheese, starry sky.

Rainforest Dwellers

Huddled together at night,
        the white-naped mangebey troupe
                with curling sideburns and surprised white eyelids
                    will go when the strip of forest goes;
vanishing, too, the whitebellied shortwing flycatchers
        with their thin whistles and high-pitched songs,
                the few remaining lion-tailed macaques
                    with their silver manes, tool-making fingers,
and the Nilgiri langurs, hunted as aphrodisiacs,
        whose whoops echo through the dark branches—
                those remnant cloud-catchers whose leaves
                seed the rain.

And we, descended a million years from forest
        to those at glacier's edge who made oil lamps
                and manganese chalk thirty thousand years ago
                    and traced, deep in the rock of France,
the procession of mastodon, mammoth, cave bear, auroch,
        and eohippus swallowed up by earth, do we too
                not carry the memory of forest life, echo
                    of each other's voices through the trees?
Before the snows came, and the ice.
        Before we were broken apart into isolate bands.
                Before the droughts came, and the sea.

Pygmy Hippopotamus

(Hexaprotodon liberiensis)

Small as hippos go, pig-size;
nostrils low, sweat oiling their gray-green skin—
two or three thousand left on the planet
in Liberia's swampy forests, prized for their tusks
and bushmeat.

River-horse, relative of whale;
trail maker, late-day and night feeder
on succulents, roots, shoots, grasses,
fallen fruit, aquatic plants.

Fed, in the zoos, herbivore pellets, apples,
kale and bamboo. *Are they friendly?*
ask the children, thinking of piglets:
but no, aggressive in protecting their territory
with large sharp teeth. They open their mouths
not to yawn but to warn you away; move
to inside quarters as the temperature drops.

When large-scale logging
and subsistence hunting end their like
on earth, what will we lose?
                                        Their babies,
born singly, the weight of our newborns,
their snuffling through the swampy routes
they've rooted out, their 30-to-50 year lives;
the stories locals tell of a mystical creature
that carries a shining stone in its mouth
to light its solitary way, with a skin so slippery
it can't be caught.

Slender Loris

(Loris tardigradus)

Brown-furred creature of white-furrowed brow,
headlamp eyes, chipmunk-size,
nose a heart-shaped blob,
eating a red flower in the thorny dark
in India's southeastern Ghats,
hunting the acacia ants
whose bites make the arm go numb,
toxic beetles and roaches.
Wipe hands in its urine
to neutralize the stings.

Magical in every part, say some,
one loris held in the hand worth a year's salary.
Its huge eyes cooked with herbs, an aphrodisiac,
flesh a cure for wheezing asthma,
skin and toenails dried for good-luck charms.
Live voodoo doll, caged and tortured
in whatever part we wish our enemy to hurt;
its power passed on to village buyers
by threads we place in its hands.

The few left now
gather at changing light in the remote
forest canopy to play, to groom,
mothers carrying babies,
moving carefully, easily startled, alert.
And when the thread of the forest goes,
vanishing too will be its power
to bring down the rain, to hold the soil,
to shelter tiny worried bodies
holding to branches, eyes big in the dark.

Yangtze Basin River Dolphin

(Yangtze Baiji, *Lipotes vexillifer*)

Only thirteen like you,
sighted ten years ago, in the river
where 400 million people
try to make their living,
dynamiting open the sewage-filled channels,
building dams, catching fish with rolling hooklines, gill nets,
electric stun guns; so many boats that they collide—
already in the river too muddy to see you,
the latest count says you are gone,
repeating the loss of legend—

that once you were a beautiful princess,
drowned by your father for refusing to marry
a man you did not love—

you who carried your calf
close to the side of your body,
diving and breathing, clicking and calling
to the rest of your kind—reincarnate again
in the songs of the doomed and shot and drowned,
last passenger pigeon of water,
another creature we could not love.

Harlequin Frogs of the Cloud Forest Preserve, Costa Rica

Say you lived in mist, near streams,
    your red toes grasping hard
        the slippery stems of things.
           Say your voice made rain.

And say your kind are dying—
    the warmer nights breeding
        a killing fungus; or that the rain
          is poisoned now.

Say silence falls, a disappearing.
    And though you shine in your bright skin
        in the photograph, though you are the music
          in this poem, say elegy is not enough—

it's the triage of the battlefield
    we should be making—the whining ambulance,
        emergency medic who packs you up
          in his suitcase

and smuggles you into his research lab, an ark,
    with his eye on the slides under the microscope
        and his voice loud
          and his haste palpable.

V. Beginning Again

Praying to the God of Leavetakings

You who stand outside the flood of time and landscapes' fractal hills
to witness what escapes, mathematician of leavetakings that endlessly
repeat, decay, what prayer should we make? You outside the multiverse
with eyes to see every fallen thing, each sparrow dropping in the talons
of the sparrowhawk, each branched old-growth tree emptying the canopy,
each handful of red rock the river bears away, each of us in the grip
of great old age or sudden accident, each galaxy spiraling into the dark,
central, hungry black; you who see all forms, stones, stars falling away,
departures in kaleidoscope display—teach us to invert your sight,
to see, in our small span, the bright, brief presence of the living.

Beginning Again in Banff

Begin in the body
taking in *sun, snow, tracks,*
the lodgepole trunks

body whose every cell
speaks to its neighbors,
the roaming bands

of T-cells, lymphocytes,
peptides, transmitters,
fired off by sight of sky,

each cell's spool
of protein machinery
wound by local tides

to offer a few words
to be read each hour
in the push and pull

of memory—body-mind
looking back through
its slosh of history—

begin in the body,
eye and touch,
nerve and gut,

listening
to itself lighting up
in the clouds' alpine glow.

In the Teeth of the Wind

The red squirrel does not carry
       the world in her teeth. She carries
       pine cones to a high branch to eat and sheds
       new trees. She recycles the cabin's
       pink foam insulation to her nest
       for days of minus forty.

The red-breasted nuthatches' small patches
       of red and slate blue
       are the only color in this black and white world
       of lodgepoles and snow. They do not carry
       the world in their wings. They grub out
       the larvae of pinebark beetles,
       alter death's calligraphy.

The mule deer does not carry
       the world on her back. She keeps
       close track of her twin fawns,
       leads them down the ravine
       to green browse.

The trees do not carry
       the world on their backs—
       the back of the world carries them,
       tall columns of carbon storage, oxygen pumps,
       fuel, say the resource books.

Children
       do not carry the world on their backs—
       they play among stumps, or the rubble
       of a mountain top leveled for coal
       and dumped in the creeks.

In the teeth of the wind
       I ask what we can dream,
       how each depends on each.
       Even the words scrawled
       on this page to reach you.

Joe's Dream

Not Goethe's big dream with its power
to move the hearts of men but a small one
of feeding a child in the Gambian village
of children where the oldest is fifteen
and many have HIV—and Pastor Joe,
who lives in DeKalb, the middle of the USA
where taxes eat up the farmers
and developers eat up the land, looks out
at the acres waiting for bobcats and asphalt
and McMansions as the builders raise cash
and sees fallow fields that could, for the two
or three years in between, raise grain;
talks the planners into short-term land-loan,
scavenges seed from the grain silos,
recruits the ex-farmer, in real estate now,
and church friends to till and sow 80 acres of wheat
that will complete the protein needed in Gambia,
where the children are being taught to grow
fruits and vegetables—Joe looks out
at emptiness and hunger
and dreams a small, short-term, doable dream.

All that breathing out we do–

adopt a row of indoor house plants, then
plant a tree for every car, whitewash
the parking lot, convert it weekly
to local farmers' market, walk,
turn down your thermostat,
shingle roofs with solar cells,
replace your incandescents, surround
the steam plants with acres of hybrid
poplars that grow six feet a year,
or willow rampant in southern heat,
switchgrass thriving in arid plains—
burn them clean, carbon-neutral,
return the ash to fertilize the soil,
rotate crops, contour plow—and don't stop
there—at the Gobi's edge, plant the line
of trees that will hold the soil, water weekly,
then next year a new row for a new
Great Wall, believe one person
makes a difference—already
my rubber plant has doubled,
one woman in our midwestern town
has reroofed with solar shingles
and linked to the electric power grid,
a retired engineer is testing poplars out,
and far away in the Gobi, a man walks
the first mile of trees, carrying a bucket
from dawn to dusk.

Cassandra Looks at Dark Matter
Through Hubble's Eye

Winter again, and all that futile calling out
against the specters of lost childhoods, famines,
greed and drought, wars and terror
quiets, as, putting her eye to Hubble's past light,
thoughts of hurling herself over a cliff subside,
replaced by the faint shape of what's been missed:
the unseen mass of the universe that aligns
our fears, brought into focus by gravity's lens.
Beneath each fear its antidote: the pull
of the lovely lumpiness of life.
The beautiful archaic blues of the night sky
lit by stars and moon, the glitter and shine of snow,
the long patience of trees, and on each face
on our path the joy of watching
the fawn sleep, the pine marten play.

Field Sparrow

Her small grass cup
  bulges with four gray babies,
their popeyes shut, bony wings folded,
  yolky beaks agape,
underfoot in the field
  of goldenrod and turkey grass
as she hangs on the juniper's
  drooping tip–
a few stalks of grass
  between her blind brood
and the circling hawk.
  In the field of her being,
in the field of her making,
  in the field of her future,
she sings and sings.

Time-Lapse

The Arabidopsis seedling's small root tip
probes the rock in its path, tests for crevice, gap,
twists to travel sideways along the granite face
to the next loose texture of crumbly soil where it turns,
growing once again down, and down,
and down to the end of the video clip, its tip
protected by capsule cells, and behind, four more
that store starch granules whose weight
tumbles to tell the root the direction of gravity's pull—
clues spoken to some relay system of molecules
that translate into calls for walls to lengthen growth
this side or that as wave after wave of calcium
spreads back in green fluorescence, signaling
the shimmering explosive push of life that thrums
along the root tip's lengthening stretch, the root hairs
bursting out right-angled a little way back: there,
speeded up, the urgent intelligence of every cell.

The All of It √

The universe is modeled there
on the NASA computer screen
against a dark blue backdrop of ignorance—
all we know of space,
all we've had of time:
a drinking glass with a flaring rim
on a wobbly base, that blip
where we began inflating
from sub-atomic scale to grapefruit size
in the first trillion-trillionth of a second—
so says the three-year scan
of the background radiation
still pulsing in the star map—
a glass of time, holding a small level
of espresso dark, and then the early stars,
fusion furnaces turning on,
and later yet the Milky Way,
and rotating about a minor sun,
a rock with water on it
where now we peer about
in the quantum foam—
and then the widening lip
where one day time will spill us out
and no lip of ours can stoop to drink again
the knowledge of that spring.
Still, the dark blue backdrop
offers hope of god or natural law
where beginnings are small enough
to hold us all, the way the mind
can hold the drinking glass
or the newborn child
that love set going
from incomplete halves.

Genevieve at Twelve Months

While children hurl dried grass
into the bonfire and ash drifts over us,
Genevieve hunkers down,
concentrates, rises; wobbles
to her feet,
steps forward
for the first time
into this world where we forget
the amazement of standing up,
of lifting a foot,
pushing off, falling toward earth
and catching ourselves
over and over again.

What luck

           to be tuned to this fraction
of spectrum we see as *rainbow, rainbow,*

that our two small ear-drums
move to the hum of another's voice,

those twin stretched membranes
vibrating resonant with breath,

that these gyroscopes of our inner ear
track our cartwheels when gravity tugs,

that our tongues taste honey and salt.
What luck that we can smell the rain,

that these hands can touch, cradle,
caress this skin that enfolds us

all our days—what luck to be born
root and blossom and branch of life

into this world we're shaped to—
to tremble in its flux

with the hunting hawk, the mouse
the layered rocks, the eelgrass meadow.

THE TEBOT BACH MISSION

The mission of Tebot Bach is to strengthen community, to promote literacy, to broaden the audience for poetry by community outreach programs and publishing, and to demonstrate the power of poetry to transform life experiences through readings, workshops and publications.

THE TEBOT BACH PROGRAMS

1. A poetry reading and writing workshop series for venues which serve marginalized populations such as homeless shelters, battered women's and men's shelters, nursing homes, senior citizen daycare centers, Veterans organizations, hospitals, AIDS hospices, and correctional facilities, and for schools K-College. Participating poets include: John Balaban, M.I. Liebler, Patricia Smith, Dorianne Laux, Laurence Lieberman, Richard Jones, Arthur Sze and Carol Moldaw.

2. A poetry reading and writing workshop series for the community of Southern California at large. The workshops feature local, national, and international teaching poets. Participating poets include: David St. John, Charles Webb, Wanda Coleman, Amy Gerstler, Patricia Smith, Holly Prado, Dorothy Barresi, W.D. Ehrhart, Tom Lux, Rebecca Seiferle, Suzanne Lummis, Michael Datcher, B.H. Fairchild, Cecilia Woloch, Chris Abani, Laurel Ann Bogen, Sam Hamill, David Lehman, and Mark Doty.

3. A publishing component in order to give local, national, and international poets a venue for publishing and distribution.

Grateful acknowledgement is given to Steve and Lera B. Smith, our donors, and to Golden West College in Huntington Beach, California, all of whom make our programs possible.

TEBOT BACH
HUNTINGTON BEACH • CALIFORNIA
WWW.TEBOTBACH.ORG